A Cat Butt Birthday is like a regular birthday but better!

Cat Butts love the same things about birthdays as you do: cake, candles, party hats, piñatas, balloons... and in this book you'll get to color all of these and more!

Grab the crayons and markers, and join forces with your Cat Butt-loving friends for a most unique coloring experience.

Who knows, maybe you'll get some new ideas for your next birthday party!

CAT BUTT BIRTHDAY!

A COLORING BOOK

© VALBRAINS 2018

@ValBrains & valbrains.com

#icoloredcatbutts

BALLOON BUTT

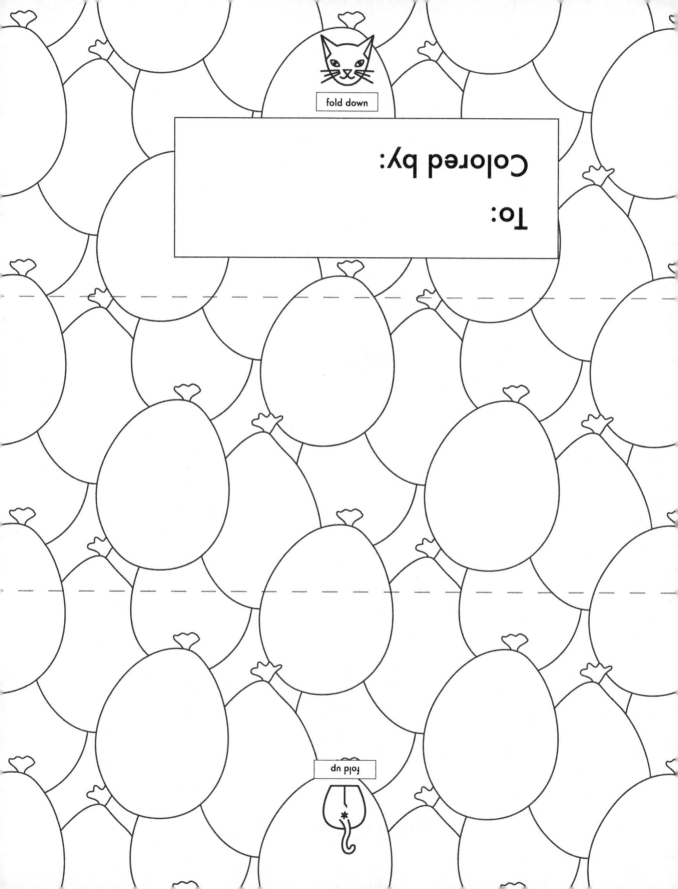

fold down

To: Colored by:

fold up

MAKE A WISH!

fold down

To:

Colored by:

fold up

PUT A CAT BUTT ON IT

fold down

Colored by:

To:

fold up

B IS FOR BUTT!

fold down

To:

Colored by:

fold up

I MADE YOU SOMETHING

fold down

Colored by:

To:

fold up

BIRTHDAY BUNS

fold down

To:

Colored by:

fold up

PURRRFECT GIFT

fold down

To:

Colored by:

fold up

CAT BUTT CLOWN SURPRISE!

fold down

To: Colored by:

fold up

DONUT HOLES

fold down

Colored by:

To:

fold up

CAT BUTT HOW-TO

fold down

To:

Colored by:

fold up

BUTTLOONS

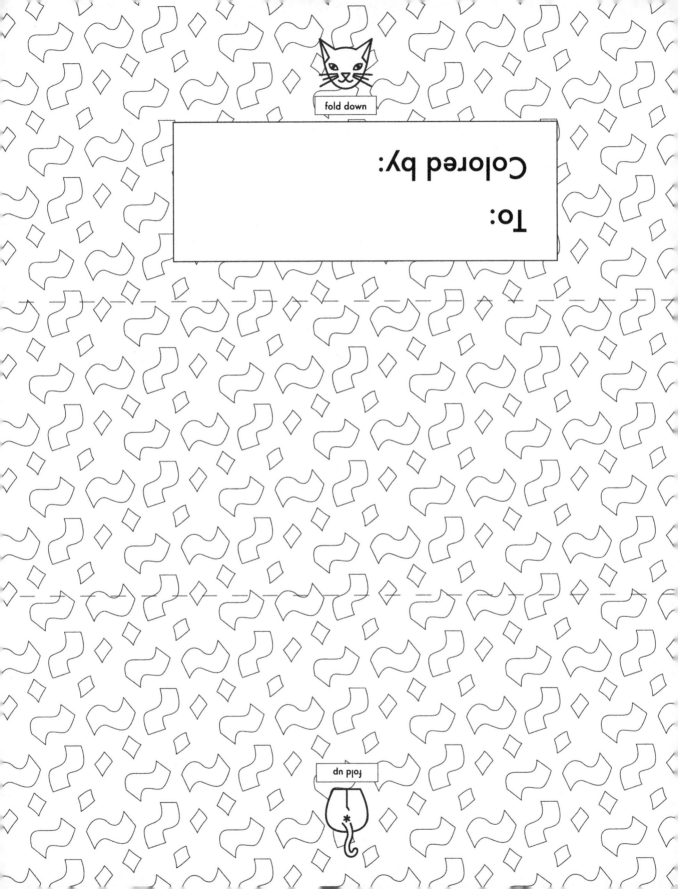

fold down

To:

Colored by:

fold up

COORDINATING CAT BUTTS

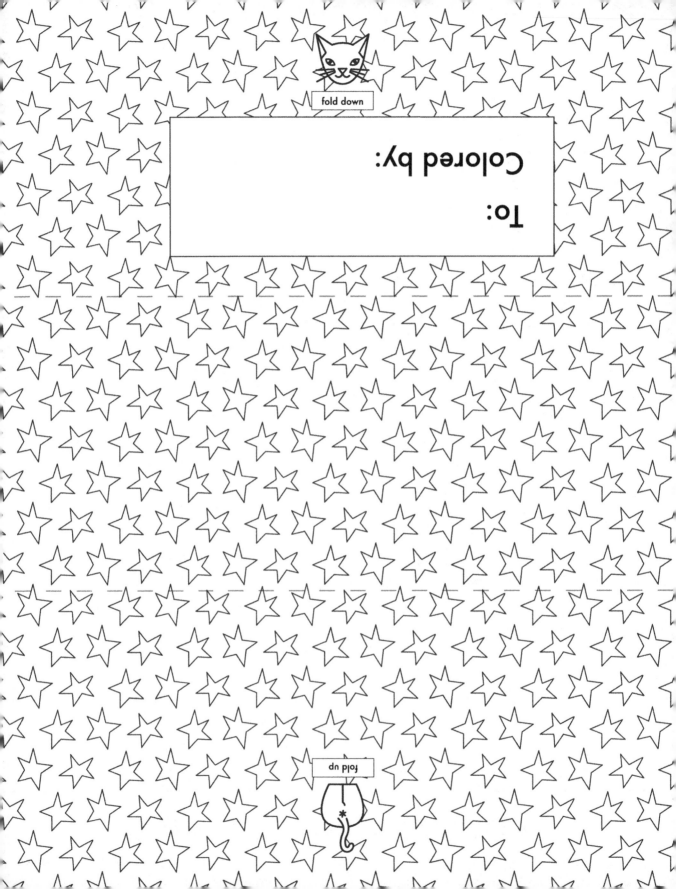

fold down

To: Colored by:

fold up

CAT BUTT B-DAY BUNDLE

fold down

Colored by:

To:

fold up

CAT BUTT CANDLE!

fold down

Colored by:

To:

fold up

SURPRISE CAT BUTT!

fold down

Colored by:

To:

fold up

CAT BUTT PIÑATA

fold down

To:

Colored by:

fold up

CAT BUTT PIZZA PARTY!!!

fold down

To: Colored by:

fold up

PIN THE TAIL ON THE CAT BUTT

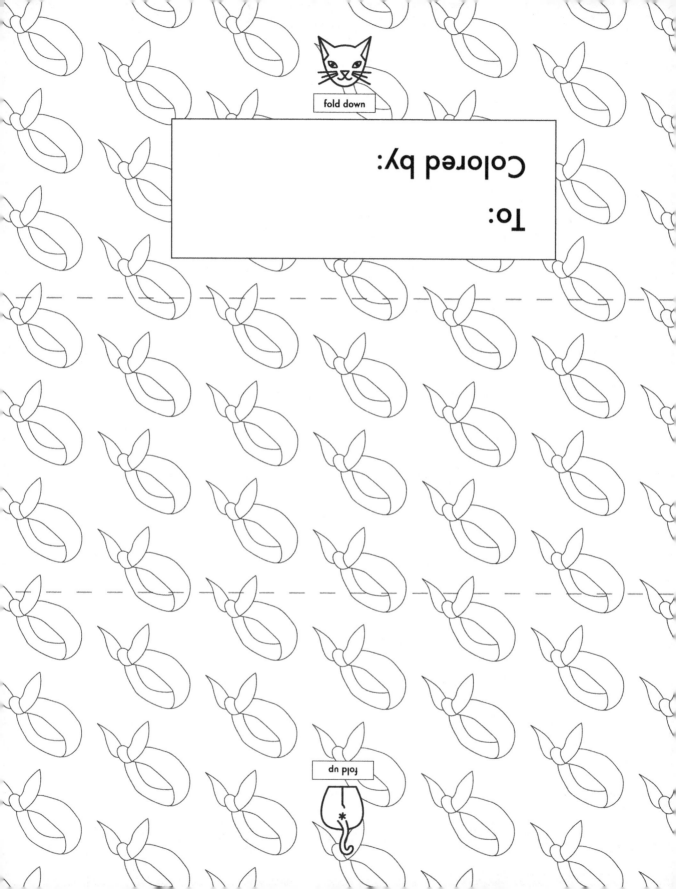

fold down

To: Colored by:

fold up

DISGRUNTLED CAT (BUTT)

fold down

To:

Colored by:

fold up

KATRAOKE

fold down

To:

Colored by:

fold up

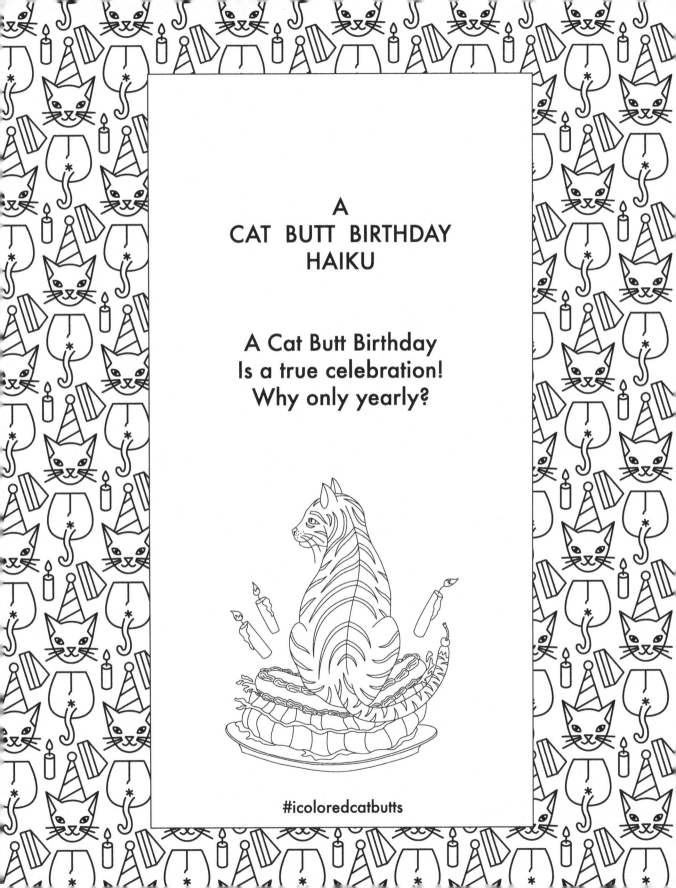

A
CAT BUTT BIRTHDAY
HAIKU

A Cat Butt Birthday
Is a true celebration!
Why only yearly?

#icoloredcatbutts

Made in the USA
Columbia, SC
17 July 2019